The Day at the Shore and the Octopus Lure

PAMELA LEBLANC
Illustrated by : Pumudi Gardiyawasam

Copyrights © 2021 By Pamela LeBlanc
Illustrated By Pumudi Gardiyawasam

No part of this book may be reproduced or transmitted in any form without the written premission of the Author except for the use of quotations in a book review.

Dedication

This is, lovingly, dedicated to my parents
who always encouraged me to follow my heart.
And, to my Son
who has already begun following his.

We ran to the kitchen to chop, slice and dice.
A picnic without food just wouldn't be nice!

We had pickles, cheese and crackers galore.
And crumbs for the fishies - it's what they adore.
We packed melon and cherries and MORE healthy treats.
So, why on earth do I keep dreaming of sweets?

A week ago, or maybe more, I hid IT inside my secret drawer.
I was saving IT for a special day but what could be better than a day at the bay?
I tucked IT inside my hide-a-way-pocket and
shot down the stairs with the speed of a rocket.

Tell NO one, I thought. It will all be for me.
I'll treasure it, admire it and eat it with glee.

It's swirly and slurpy and amazingly good. You'd hide it too.
You KNOW you would!
It's round and delicious and sticky like glue.
IT'S a big YUMMY sucker in red, white and blue.

We jumped in the car and set off for the beach,
wind in my face, sucker just out of reach.
I don't know what's better or what's worth more,
my precious treat or a day at the shore.

IT and me leapt into the sea
for some sugary licks to my absolute glee!

What I saw in the water set off my alarms.
A purple-pink BLOB with eight grabby arms.

Before I knew what to do or to say,
its little pink tentacle snatched IT away!

The octopus was thrilled with her newfound treasure.
She splashed and she jiggled in absolute pleasure.

As she danced and pranced, her smile twisted in greed,
I spotted two CREEPY eyes from beneath the seaweed!
While Octo was laughing and doing a jig
those eyes got WAY closer and those eyes were WAYYY big!

It was a big shark and, boy, he was hungry!
He hadn't had a bite since Sunday or Monday.
Octo saw the mean gleam in his eye.
So, she tried to escape. And, OH, so did I.

But, Sharky was smart. And, Sharky was quick.
He bit into that sucker lickity split.

Now, I won't fight a shark for my prized IT!
I don't like shark teeth,
Or, shark breath, Or, shark spit.

My mind said "BACK UP" and my legs said "RUN"!
When, out came a claw that pinched Sharky's bum!

"EEEEYYYYOOOWWW" cried Sharky as he dropped my fair treat.
It sank to the bottom near Lobby's red feet.

"OH JOY" Lobby screamed as he scurried away
He had never tasted candy on a stick this way!

But, sure as sure could ever be,
this was NOT the end of the battle at sea!

There lay my sucker all licked by too many and now just as dirty as a 10-year-old penny.

At this point I am feeling incredibly bad.
Not scared and not mad.
Just, dreadfully, SAD!

I started to cry. A series of wails!
While the sea creatures stared and tucked in their tails.
They'd been too distracted by the fight for the treat
to notice they were next to a beast with two feet!

This beast was getting extremely scary!
All RED. And ANGRY. And STOMPY. And HAIRY.
As the sea creatures stared at this monster in fright,
they scattered and swam and scurried for life!

The battle was over but **NOBODY** won.
My sucker was broken, all licked and half done!
As I bent down to pick up my sad looking IT,
I noticed that Octo came back for a bit.

I wanted to scream. I wanted to SHOUT.
But then she extended her tentacle out.

Was she giving me something? I couldn't quite tell.
But that's when I saw the pearl in the shell.
She stuffed HER prized IT in my hide-away-pocket.
A "sorry" for the battle and being unable to stop it.

She surfaced the ocean and gave me a nod.
And, gracefully, swam off with her family pod.

NOBODY would believe a story so wild!
That I made friends with an octo-child!
From that day on, and forever more,
there would never be a better day at the shore.